Maui Travel guide

The most up to date pocket guide and tips to planning Yourself to Maui.

Peyton Jack

Labour day (1st Monday in September).
Veterans day (November 11).
Thanksgiving day (4 Thursday in September).
Most attractive cities in maui and histories.
Chapter 5
General security solutions.
Crime rates in maui.
Emergency and important numbers you must know.
Police emergency 911
Fire emergency 911
Medical emergency 911
Police department.
Maui memorial medical center.
U S coast guard.
Maui stations.
Entertainment in maui.
Roles of Maui governments towards the immigrant.
What you must do before leaving Maui.
Conclusions.

Chapter 1

<u>Hello, you are welcome to Maui the city of wonder's.</u>

Traveling to Maui is a remarkable experience that leaves visitors with lasting memories and a sense of awe. This beautiful Hawaiian island offers a diverse range of natural wonders, cultural attractions, and recreational activities that cater to all types of travelers. Whether you're seeking adventure, relaxation, or immersion in local traditions, Maui has it all.

One of the highlights of visiting Maui is exploring its breathtaking landscapes. From the lush rainforests of the Road to Hana to the jaw-dropping views of Haleakala National Park, the island's natural beauty is truly awe-inspiring. Witnessing a sunrise or sunset atop the Haleakala volcano is a must-do experience that will leave you speechless.

Maui is also renowned for its pristine beaches, offering visitors the opportunity to unwind and soak up the sun. From the world-famous Kaanapali Beach with its golden sands and crystal-clear waters to the secluded shores of Makena Beach, there's a beach for every preference. Snorkeling and scuba diving enthusiasts will be delighted by the vibrant underwater ecosystems and the chance to swim alongside sea turtles and colorful tropical fish.

The island's rich cultural heritage is another captivating aspect of a trip to Maui. The local Hawaiian culture is deeply rooted in the island's history, and there are numerous opportunities to engage with it. Visit the small town of Lahaina, once the capital of the Hawaiian Kingdom, to explore its historic landmarks and vibrant art scene. Attend a traditional luau to savor Hawaiian cuisine, witness hula dancing, and learn about ancient customs and legends.

Adventure seekers will find no shortage of thrilling activities in Maui. The island is a paradise for water sports enthusiasts, offering opportunities for surfing, paddleboarding, kayaking, and even whale watching during the winter months. For those seeking a more adrenaline-fueled experience, embarking on a helicopter tour over Maui's dramatic landscapes or trying out zip-lining in the lush valleys are popular choices.

Food lovers will also be delighted by Maui's culinary scene. From fresh seafood caught daily to farm-to-table dining experiences, the island offers a diverse range of flavors. Sample traditional Hawaiian dishes like poke and kalua pork, or indulge in fusion cuisine that combines local ingredients with international influences.

In conclusion, traveling to Maui is an unforgettable experience that caters to all types of travelers. Whether you're seeking natural wonders, cultural immersion, adventure, or simply a chance to relax on stunning beaches, Maui has something for everyone. The island's beauty, diverse activities, and warm Hawaiian hospitality make it a dream destination that will leave you with cherished memories for years to come.

The location

Maui is an island located in the Central Pacific Ocean and is part of the Hawaiian archipelago. It is the second-largest island in Hawaii, both in terms of land area and population. Maui covers an area of approximately 727 square miles (1,883 square kilometers) and has a population of around 144,400 people as of 2021.

Geographically, Maui is situated about 2,400 miles (3,860 kilometers) southwest of the continental United States. It lies between the islands of Molokai and Big Island and is approximately 30 miles (48 kilometers) northwest of the island of Lanai. The island is known for its diverse landscapes, ranging from lush rainforests and cascading waterfalls to pristine beaches and volcanic formations.

Maui can be divided into several distinct regions, each offering its own unique attractions:

West Maui: This region is characterized by stunning coastal cliffs, picturesque beaches, and the historic town of Lahaina. It is home to popular attractions such as the Kaanapali Beach Resort area, where visitors can enjoy beautiful sandy beaches and luxury resorts.

South Maui: Known for its beautiful white-sand beaches and crystal-clear waters, South Maui is a popular destination for beach lovers and water sports enthusiasts. The towns of Kihei and Wailea offer a range of accommodations, restaurants, and shopping opportunities.

Upcountry Maui: Located on the slopes of Haleakala, Upcountry Maui offers a cooler climate and breathtaking views of the island. The region is known for its agricultural activities, including flower farms and the production of Maui's renowned coffee. The quaint towns of Makawao and Kula are worth exploring for their charming boutiques and art galleries.

East Maui: This area is dominated by the lush and scenic Road to Hana, a winding coastal road that stretches approximately 52 miles (84 kilometers) and offers spectacular views of waterfalls, rainforests, and dramatic seascapes. The road is dotted with numerous stops, including the Seven Sacred Pools, Wailua Falls, and the Garden of Eden Arboretum.

Central Maui: The town of Kahului serves as the main commercial hub of the island, housing Maui's main airport and harbor. It offers a range of shopping centers, restaurants, and cultural attractions like the Maui Arts and Cultural Center. Nearby, visitors can explore the historic town of Wailuku, known for its charming old buildings and local shops.

One of the most iconic landmarks on Maui is the Haleakala National Park, located in East Maui. Haleakala is a dormant volcano and its summit reaches an elevation of 10,023 feet (3,055 meters) above sea level. The park offers stunning vistas, hiking trails, and the opportunity to witness breathtaking sunrises or sunsets above the clouds.

Maui's natural beauty, rich culture, and recreational opportunities make it a sought-after destination for tourists from around the world. Whether you're looking to relax on pristine beaches, explore lush rainforests, indulge in water sports, or immerse yourself in Hawaiian traditions, Maui offers a diverse range of experiences for every visitor.

The geography

Maui is the second-largest island in the Hawaiian archipelago, located in the central Pacific Ocean. It is part of the state of Hawaii and is situated approximately 2,400 miles (3,900 kilometers) southwest of the United States mainland. Maui covers a total land area of 727 square miles (1,883 square kilometers) and is known for its diverse and stunning geography.

Maui's geography is characterized by a combination of rugged mountains, lush valleys, beautiful beaches, and volcanic features. The island was formed by the eruption of two shield volcanoes, West Maui Mountain and Haleakala, which are responsible for its unique landscape.

West Maui Mountain: Located on the northwest side of the island, West Maui Mountain is an eroded shield volcano that forms the western part of Maui. It is characterized by steep sea cliffs, deep valleys, and sharp ridges. The highest peak in West Maui Mountain is Puu Kukui, reaching an elevation of 5,788 feet (1,764 meters).

Haleakala: Situated on the eastern part of the island, Haleakala is a dormant volcano that forms the eastern half of Maui. The volcano's summit, also known as Haleakala Crater, rises to an impressive height of 10,023 feet (3,055 meters) above sea level. It is renowned for its stunning sunrises and sunsets, and the surrounding area is a national park that attracts visitors from around the world.

Central Valley: The isthmus between West Maui Mountain and Haleakala forms a fertile central valley known as the 'Valley Isle.' This area is home to a significant portion of Maui's population and is known for its agricultural activities. The valley is characterized by lush green fields, including sugarcane, pineapple, and various other crops.

Coastal Areas: Maui boasts a diverse coastline with beautiful beaches, rocky shores, and stunning cliffs. Popular coastal destinations include Lahaina, Kaanapali, Kihei, Wailea, and Hana. The island's beaches offer opportunities for swimming, snorkeling, surfing, and other water activities.

Rainforests and Waterfalls: Maui's windward side, particularly the eastern part of the island, is known for its lush rainforests and picturesque waterfalls. The Hana Highway, a scenic road along the northeastern coast, provides access to numerous waterfalls, including the famous Wailua Falls and Seven Sacred Pools.

Molokini Crater: Located off the southwestern coast of Maui, Molokini is a partially submerged volcanic crater. It is a popular destination for snorkeling and diving due to its crystal-clear waters and abundant marine life.

The climate of Maui is generally mild and tropical. The island experiences trade winds that help to keep temperatures comfortable throughout the year. The eastern side of the island, influenced by the northeast trade winds, tends to be wetter and greener, while the western side is drier and sunnier. The higher elevations, particularly in Haleakala, can be cooler and experience occasional frost or snow during the winter months.

In conclusion, Maui's geography offers a breathtaking mix of volcanic peaks, fertile valleys, stunning coastlines, and natural wonders. From the dramatic cliffs of West Maui Mountain to the majestic summit of Haleakala and the beautiful beaches that surround the island, Maui is a paradise for outdoor enthusiasts and nature lovers alike.

The demographic

Maui is the second-largest island in the state of Hawaii, located in the Central Pacific Ocean. It is part of Maui County, which also includes the islands of Molokai and Lanai. Maui is known for its stunning natural beauty, diverse landscapes, and vibrant culture. Let's delve into the demographics of this enchanting island.

Population:
As of my knowledge cutoff in September 2021, the estimated population of Maui was around 167,207. It's important to note that population figures may have changed since then, and you might want to refer to updated sources for the most current information.

Ethnicity and Race:
The population of Maui is diverse, reflecting the multicultural nature of Hawaii. The major ethnic groups on the island include:

Native Hawaiians and Pacific Islanders: Native Hawaiians are the indigenous people of the Hawaiian Islands, and they have a significant presence on Maui.

Pacific Islanders from various Polynesian islands also contribute to the ethnic makeup of the island.

Asians: People of Asian descent, including Japanese, Filipino, Chinese, Korean, and Vietnamese, have a notable presence on Maui. Many individuals from these communities have migrated to the island and have contributed to its cultural fabric.

Caucasians: Caucasians, mainly of European ancestry, make up a portion of the population, with many being descendants of early settlers and immigrants who arrived in the 19th and 20th centuries.

Hispanics and Latinos: The Hispanic and Latino community has grown over the years on Maui, contributing to the island's diversity.

Other ethnicities: There are also smaller populations representing other ethnic backgrounds, including African Americans, Native Americans, and individuals from other parts of the world.

Religion:
Religion plays a significant role in the lives of many people on Maui. The major religions practiced on the island include Christianity (various denominations), Buddhism, and other Asian religions. Additionally, traditional Hawaiian spiritual practices and beliefs are still observed by some Native Hawaiians.

Maui, also known as Māui, is a figure from Polynesian mythology and folklore, particularly prominent in the cultures of the Pacific islands, including Hawaii, Tahiti, and New Zealand. Although Maui is not considered a religion in itself, the stories and legends surrounding Maui have a significant religious and cultural impact on the indigenous peoples of these regions. In this response, I will provide you with a detailed overview of the mythology and religious aspects associated with Maui.

Mythology and Legends of Maui:

Maui is a demigod or a hero in Polynesian mythology, renowned for his extraordinary deeds and mischievous nature. He is often depicted as a skilled fisherman, navigator, and shapeshifter, with a strong connection to the natural elements. The tales of Maui vary across different Polynesian cultures, but they share common themes and characteristics.

Creation and Genealogy:

In many versions of the mythology, Maui is considered the son of the god Tangaroa, who is associated with the sea. Maui's mother is usually Hina, a goddess or a mortal woman. Maui is often depicted as having several brothers, including Māui-taha, Māui-roto, Māui-pae, and Māui-waho.

Key Deeds and Exploits:

Maui is best known for his incredible feats and adventures. Some of his notable accomplishments include:

Fishing Up Islands: One of the most well-known stories depicts Maui using a magical fish hook made from the jawbone of his ancestor to fish up the islands from the depths of the ocean. This act played a significant role in the creation of the Pacific islands.

Slowing the Sun: In another legend, Maui sets out to slow down the sun to make the days longer and give people more time to work. He achieved this by restraining the sun with ropes or by standing on Mount Haleakala in Hawaii and using his supernatural powers.

Battle with the Sun: Maui is also credited with capturing and taming the sun. In some versions, he accomplished this by ensnaring the sun in ropes and beating it until it agreed to move more slowly across the sky, leading to longer daylight hours.

Obtaining Fire: Maui is believed to have stolen fire from the underworld and gifted it to humanity, bringing warmth, light, and the ability to cook food.

Journey to the Underworld: In one legend, Maui ventures into the realm of the gods and battles various supernatural beings to gain immortality for humankind. However, he ultimately meets his demise in the process.

Religious and Cultural Significance:
The stories and legends surrounding Maui hold immense religious and cultural significance for the indigenous peoples of Polynesia. They often serve as a way to explain natural phenomena, the origins of the islands, and human existence. Maui's exploits are seen as demonstrations of human potential, bravery, and ingenuity.

In addition to his role as a mythological hero, Maui is sometimes revered as a cultural hero or even a god in certain regions. He is considered a guardian of fishermen and associated with fishing rituals, as well as a protector of navigation and voyaging. Maui is also regarded as a symbol of resilience, adaptability, and the power of the human spirit to overcome challenges.

Worship and Rituals:
While there is no organized religion solely dedicated to worshiping Maui, his stories and legends are often incorporated into the religious practices and rituals of Polynesian cultures. These rituals may involve offering prayers, chants, or invocations to Maui, particularly during fishing expeditions or seafaring journeys. Some cultural festivals and ceremonies celebrate Maui's exploits, promoting cultural preservation and a sense of community.

Age Distribution:
The age distribution on Maui, like many other places, is diverse. It includes individuals of all age groups, from young children to older adults. However, specific age group data may vary, and up-to-date sources can provide more detailed information.

<u>Economy</u>:
Maui's economy is primarily driven by tourism, agriculture, and small businesses. The tourism industry plays a significant role in providing employment opportunities and driving economic growth on the island. Agriculture includes the cultivation of crops such as sugarcane, pineapple, coffee, and tropical fruits. Additionally, the arts and crafts industry, along with local businesses, contributes to the island's economy.

Maui's demographics reflect a vibrant mix of cultures and ethnicities, creating a diverse and culturally rich environment. The population's composition and dynamics may have evolved since my knowledge cutoff in September 2021, so it's advisable to refer to current sources for the most accurate and up-to-date information on the demographic profile of Maui.

<u>The language</u>

The people of Maui, an island in the state of Hawaii, primarily speak English as their official language.

English is the language of instruction in schools, used in government and legal proceedings, and widely spoken in business and tourism. However, it is important to note that there is a rich cultural and linguistic heritage in Maui that extends beyond English.

One of the prominent languages in Maui is Hawaiian, the ancestral language of the indigenous Polynesian people who inhabited the islands before the arrival of Europeans. Hawaiian is a Polynesian language, and it is closely related to other Polynesian languages such as Tahitian, Samoan, and Maori. The Hawaiian language is considered an official language in the state of Hawaii alongside English, and efforts have been made to revitalize and preserve it.

Historically, Hawaiian was the primary language spoken by the native population of Maui. It was used in daily communication, storytelling, chants, and songs. However, the suppression of the Hawaiian language during the 19th and early 20th centuries led to a significant decline in fluency and usage. Hawaiian language education was banned in schools, and generations of Hawaiians were discouraged from speaking their native language. As a result, the number of native Hawaiian speakers dwindled, and the language was on the verge of extinction.

In recent decades, there has been a revival of interest in the Hawaiian language and efforts to reclaim and revitalize it. Hawaiian language immersion schools have been established, where children are taught all subjects in Hawaiian. These initiatives have played a crucial role in preserving and passing on the language to future generations.

While English is widely spoken on Maui, there are still pockets of the community where Hawaiian is spoken and understood. Native Hawaiians and those who have studied the language actively use Hawaiian in cultural ceremonies, hula performances, and community gatherings. Many place names, landmarks, and natural features on Maui have Hawaiian names, reflecting the enduring influence of the language.

In addition to English and Hawaiian, Maui is a diverse community with residents from various backgrounds and ethnicities. As a result, other languages are spoken on the island due to the multicultural nature of its population. For example, languages like Tagalog, Ilocano, Japanese, Chinese, Korean, and Spanish are spoken by immigrant communities or those with familial ties to other countries.

Overall, while English is the dominant language on Maui, the cultural significance and efforts to preserve Hawaiian have ensured its continued presence on the island. The linguistic diversity of the community also adds to the tapestry of languages spoken on Maui.

Chapter 2

Safety trips to Maui

Maui, located in Hawaii, is a popular destination known for its stunning beaches, lush landscapes, and vibrant culture. Planning a safe trip to Maui involves considering various aspects such as health and safety precautions, transportation, accommodation, and activities. Here is a detailed guide to help ensure a safe and enjoyable trip to Maui.

Making research and Planning:

Before your trip, conduct thorough research about Maui, including its weather, local customs, and safety guidelines. Check official websites, travel advisories, and forums for up-to-date information.
Create an itinerary based on your interests and preferences. Identify the activities and attractions you want to explore while considering safety aspects. Familiarize yourself with local laws, emergency contact numbers, and medical facilities available on the island. Health and Safety Precautions:

Consult with your healthcare provider well in advance to ensure you are up to date on routine vaccinations. They may also provide guidance on any specific vaccinations required for traveling to Maui.

Consider purchasing travel insurance that covers medical expenses, trip cancellations, and unforeseen emergencies.

Pack a well-stocked first aid kit, including any prescription medications, mosquito repellent, sunscreen, and any other personal healthcare items you may require.

Follow general health guidelines such as washing hands frequently, using hand sanitizers, and practicing proper respiratory etiquette.

Transportation:

If flying to Maui, choose reputable airlines and check their safety measures and protocols related to COVID-19 or any other health concerns.

When renting a car, ensure it is from a reliable and well-established rental agency. Familiarize yourself with the local traffic rules and signs.

If using public transportation or taxis, verify the safety protocols implemented by the service providers, such as mask requirements or limited capacity.

Accommodation:

Select accommodations with good reviews, high safety standards, and appropriate security measures.

Check if the establishment has implemented enhanced cleaning procedures in response to the COVID-19 pandemic.

Ensure your accommodation is located in a safe neighborhood with easy access to amenities and transportation options.

Water Safety:

When swimming or engaging in water activities, always follow beach safety guidelines and heed warning signs posted by lifeguards.
Only swim in designated areas with lifeguards present and avoid swimming alone.
Be cautious of strong ocean currents and riptides. If caught in one, swim parallel to the shore until you escape the current before swimming back to land.
If you are not a confident swimmer, consider wearing a life jacket or participating in water activities under professional supervision.
Outdoor Activities:

When engaging in outdoor activities such as hiking, camping, or snorkeling, ensure you are adequately prepared. Research the difficulty level, required equipment, and safety precautions for each activity.
Hike with a buddy or join organized group tours led by experienced guides, especially in remote or challenging areas.
Always stay on designated trails, follow signage, and avoid trespassing on private property.
If planning to snorkel or scuba dive, choose reputable operators with experienced instructors and proper safety equipment.
Weather Awareness:

Be aware of Maui's weather patterns and any potential hazards. Check weather forecasts regularly and pay attention to warnings or advisories issued by local authorities.

During hurricane or storm seasons (typically June to November), stay informed about any potential storms and follow instructions from local authorities.

If planning to hike or explore higher elevations, be prepared for changes in weather conditions and carry appropriate gear, including rain gear and warm clothing.

Cultural Sensitivity:

Respect the local culture and customs of Maui. Learn about the traditions, values, and etiquette of the Hawaiian people

Before traveling to Maui, it's a good idea to download a map of the island and gather other useful information to enhance your experience. Here's a detailed guide on downloading a Maui map and other things to consider:

Making use of map

There are several map applications available that offer offline maps and navigation. Two popular options are Google Maps and Maps.me. Both apps allow you to download maps for offline use and provide detailed information about points of interest, driving directions, and hiking trails.

Downloading Maps with Google Maps

Install the Google Maps app on your smartphone or tablet from the app store (available for both iOS and Android).
Open the app and search for "Maui" to display the island.
Tap on the Maui area and then tap on the "Download" button.
Select the desired map area or the entire island to download.
Once the download is complete, you can access the map offline by opening the Google Maps app and finding the downloaded map under the "Offline maps" section.
Downloading Maps with Maps.me:

Install the Maps.me app on your smartphone or tablet from the app store (available for both iOS and Android).
Open the app and search for "Maui" to display the island.
Tap on the "Download" button to download the map for the Maui area.
You can choose to download the entire island or specific regions within Maui.
After the download is finished, the map will be available for offline use in the Maps.me app.
Other Useful Information to Gather:

Apart from the map, there are other things you should consider before traveling to Maui:

Weather: Check the weather forecast for Maui during your travel dates. This will help you pack appropriate clothing and plan your activities accordingly.
Accommodation: Research and book your accommodation in advance. Maui offers a variety of options ranging from hotels and resorts to vacation rentals and campgrounds.
Transportation: Decide on your preferred mode of transportation, whether it's renting a car, using public transportation, or relying on rideshare services. Book any necessary transportation in advance.
Points of Interest: Make a list of the attractions, beaches, hiking trails, and other points of interest you want to visit on Maui. Research their opening hours, entry fees (if any), and any restrictions.
Safety Precautions: Familiarize yourself with safety guidelines and precautions specific to Maui. This includes understanding ocean safety, hiking guidelines, and respecting the local environment and culture.
By downloading a map of Maui and gathering other useful information, you'll be well-prepared to navigate the island and make the most of your trip. Remember to plan ahead, stay flexible, and enjoy the breathtaking beauty and aloha spirit of Maui!

<u>Safety tips to Maui</u>

When it comes to visiting Maui, a beautiful island in Hawaii, it's important to prioritize safety to ensure a memorable and incident-free experience. Here are some detailed safety tips to keep in mind while exploring Maui:

Water Safety:
Always check the surf conditions before swimming or engaging in water activities. Pay attention to warning signs and follow the advice of lifeguards.
Be cautious of strong currents, rip currents, and undertows. If caught in a rip current, swim parallel to the shore until you are out of the current, and then swim back to the shore.
Avoid swimming alone, especially in remote areas. It's best to swim in designated areas with lifeguards present.
If you're snorkeling or diving, be aware of your surroundings and watch out for boats. Use a dive flag to indicate your presence in the water.
Apply and regularly reapply waterproof sunscreen to protect your skin from sunburn.
Hiking and Outdoor Activities:
Before embarking on a hike, research the trail, know its difficulty level, and check the weather forecast. Inform someone about your plans and estimated return time.
Stay on marked trails and avoid venturing off into unfamiliar areas, as it can be dangerous and disturb the delicate ecosystem.

Wear appropriate footwear and clothing for hiking, and carry essentials like water, snacks, a map, a compass, and a first aid kit.

Be cautious of steep or slippery terrain, and watch out for loose rocks or tree branches that may pose a hazard.

Respect the wildlife and do not approach or feed them. Keep a safe distance from animals, especially if they are known to be dangerous.

Driving Safety:

Follow the traffic rules and regulations of Maui. Observe the speed limits and be cautious while driving on winding roads.

Use a GPS or map to familiarize yourself with the routes and plan your journeys accordingly.

Keep your vehicle locked and secure when parked. Do not leave any valuables visible inside the car.

Be mindful of pedestrians, cyclists, and motorcyclists on the road.

Avoid distracted driving, such as using your phone or eating while driving. It's best to pull over to a safe spot if you need to attend to something.

Weather Awareness:

Pay attention to weather updates and warnings issued by local authorities. Weather conditions can change quickly in Maui, so it's important to stay informed.

If there are warnings or advisories about strong winds, storms, or heavy rainfall, take them seriously and adjust your plans accordingly.

During times of heavy rain, be cautious of flash floods in low-lying areas and avoid crossing flooded roads or streams.

Respect the Environment and Local Culture:

Respect the natural beauty of Maui by disposing of your trash properly and not littering. Leave the environment as you found it to preserve its pristine state.

Be respectful of the local culture, traditions, and customs. Familiarize yourself with the local etiquette, and be mindful of sacred sites and cultural practices.

Remember, these safety tips are general guidelines, and it's important to exercise your judgment and adapt to specific situations. Stay aware of your surroundings, be prepared, and enjoy your time exploring the stunning island of Maui.

What you must know before traveling to Maui.

Traveling to Maui can be an exciting and memorable experience. Known for its stunning beaches, lush landscapes, and vibrant culture, this Hawaiian island offers a wide range of activities and attractions for visitors. However, before you embark on your journey to Maui, there are several important things to know and consider. Here's a detailed guide to help you prepare for your trip:

Travel Documents:

Valid Passport: Ensure that your passport is valid for at least six months beyond your intended stay in Maui.

Visa Requirements: Depending on your nationality, you may be eligible for visa-free entry or require a visa to enter the United States. Check the specific requirements before you travel.

Best Time to Visit:

Maui enjoys warm weather year-round, but the best time to visit is during the shoulder seasons of spring (April to May) and fall (September to November) when the crowds are smaller, and prices are more affordable. Summer (June to August) is peak tourist season, so expect larger crowds and higher prices. Winter (December to February) brings high surf and is the season for whale-watching.

Flights and Transportation:

Kahului Airport (OGG) is the main airport in Maui, located in central Maui. Many international and domestic flights operate to and from this airport.

Renting a car is highly recommended as public transportation is limited on the island. Book in advance to secure the best rates, and note that some rental companies may require drivers to be at least 25 years old.

Accommodation:

Maui offers a variety of accommodation options ranging from luxury resorts to budget-friendly hotels, vacation rentals, and bed and breakfasts. Popular areas to stay include Lahaina, Kaanapali, Kihei, and Wailea.

It's advisable to book accommodations well in advance, especially during peak travel seasons, to secure your preferred choice.

<u>**Weather and What to Pack**</u>:

Maui has a tropical climate with warm temperatures year-round. Pack lightweight and breathable clothing, such as shorts, t-shirts, sundresses, and swimsuits. Don't forget essentials like sunscreen, sunglasses, a hat, and insect repellent. If you plan on hiking or exploring Haleakala National Park, bring comfortable shoes and a light jacket for cooler temperatures at higher elevations.

Currency and Payment:

The currency used in Maui is the United States Dollar (USD). Credit cards are widely accepted, but it's a good idea to carry some cash for smaller establishments or in case of emergencies.
ATMs are available throughout the island, and major banks can be found in towns like Lahaina and Kahului.
Safety and Health:

Maui is generally a safe destination, but it's always important to take common safety precautions. Lock your car, don't leave valuables unattended on the beach, and be mindful of ocean conditions when swimming or participating in water activities.

It's recommended to purchase travel insurance to cover any medical emergencies or trip cancellations. Pack a basic first aid kit and any necessary medications.
Activities and Attractions:

Maui offers a plethora of activities to suit all interests. Don't miss visiting the iconic Road to Hana, exploring Haleakala National Park, snorkeling or scuba diving in Molokini Crater, and experiencing a traditional Hawaiian luau.
Other popular activities include surfing, stand-up paddleboarding, whale-watching (in season), visiting the Maui Ocean Center, and hiking to waterfalls in the lush rainforests.

Respect for Hawaiian Culture:

Hawaiian culture holds great significance in Maui. Respect the land and natural resources, follow any cultural protocols or guidelines at sacred sites,

Where to visit

Maui, known as the "Valley Isle," is a beautiful Hawaiian island that offers a diverse range of attractions and natural wonders. From stunning beaches and lush rainforests to majestic waterfalls and volcanic landscapes, Maui has something for everyone. Here is a detailed guide on where to visit in Maui:

Haleakala National Park: Located in the southeastern part of the island, Haleakala National Park is a must-visit destination. It is home to Haleakala, a dormant volcano with a summit that reaches over 10,000 feet. Visitors can witness breathtaking sunrises or explore the unique landscapes of the park, which include volcanic cinder cones, lunar-like deserts, and lush forests.

Road to Hana: The Road to Hana is a scenic highway that stretches along Maui's northeastern coast. The road is famous for its stunning views of the ocean, waterfalls, and lush rainforest. There are numerous stops along the way, including the Twin Falls, Bamboo Forest, Wailua Falls, and the Seven Sacred Pools at Ohe'o Gulch.

Lahaina: Lahaina is a historic town on the western coast of Maui. It was once the capital of the Hawaiian Kingdom and a bustling whaling port. Today, Lahaina is known for its vibrant art scene, quaint shops, and delicious restaurants. Visitors can explore the historic Front Street, visit the Baldwin Home Museum, or enjoy a sunset cruise from Lahaina Harbor.

Kaanapali Beach: Considered one of the best beaches in Maui, Kaanapali Beach is located just north of Lahaina. It offers soft golden sands, crystal-clear waters, and a range of water activities such as snorkeling, scuba diving, and parasailing. The beach is also lined with luxury resorts, restaurants, and shopping centers.

Iao Valley State Park: Located in Central Maui, Iao Valley State Park is a lush, scenic area known for its towering emerald-green mountains and the iconic

1,200-foot Iao Needle. Visitors can explore the park's hiking trails, learn about Hawaiian history at the park's visitor center, and enjoy picnicking in the peaceful surroundings.

Molokini Crater: A popular spot for snorkeling and diving, Molokini Crater is a partially submerged volcanic crater located just off the coast of Maui. The clear waters of the crater are home to a vibrant coral reef teeming with marine life, including colorful fish, sea turtles, and even dolphins. Excursions to Molokini Crater can be arranged from various locations on the island.

Napili Bay: Situated on Maui's northwest coast, Napili Bay is a picturesque crescent-shaped beach known for its calm waters and excellent snorkeling opportunities. The bay is surrounded by beautiful resorts and offers stunning views of neighboring islands. It's a great spot for relaxation, swimming, and soaking up the sun.

Makawao: Located in Upcountry Maui, Makawao is a charming town with a rich history in the paniolo (Hawaiian cowboy) culture. The town is known for its art galleries, boutiques, and unique shops. Visitors can explore the streets lined with colorful storefronts, enjoy a delicious meal at one of the local eateries, or attend the famous Makawao Rodeo, held annually on the Fourth of July.

These are just a few highlights of what Maui has to offer. The island is also home to numerous other stunning beaches, scenic drives, hiking trails, and cultural attractions. Whether you're seeking adventure, relaxation, or cultural experiences, Maui has something to satisfy every traveler's desires.

Chapter 3

Maui, often referred to as the "Valley Isle," is an island in the Central Pacific and one of the most sought-after destinations in Hawaii. Famous for its stunning beaches, lush landscapes, and rich cultural heritage, Maui offers a plethora of opportunities for exploration and adventure. Whether you're a nature enthusiast, water sports lover, or history buff, this tropical paradise has something to offer everyone. In this guide, we will delve into the various ways you can explore and make the most of your time on the enchanting island of Maui.

Maui's Natural Wonders:
Maui boasts an array of natural wonders that will leave you in awe. Begin your exploration by visiting Haleakalā National Park, home to the dormant Haleakalā volcano. Hike or bike through the otherworldly landscapes of the park, and if you're an early riser, witness the unforgettable sunrise from the summit.
For an extraordinary experience, embark on the Road to Hana. This scenic drive takes you along the island's northeastern coast, showcasing breathtaking waterfalls, lush rainforests, and dramatic coastal cliffs. Make sure to stop at the Garden of Eden Arboretum and the Wai'anapanapa State Park to witness the beauty of tropical flora and striking black sand beaches.

Beaches and Water Activities:
Maui's beaches are renowned for their crystal-clear waters, pristine sand, and excellent conditions for water sports. Kaanapali Beach, located on the western shore, offers a vibrant atmosphere with its luxury resorts, snorkeling spots, and opportunities for parasailing and jet skiing.
If you're seeking a more laid-back beach experience, head to the tranquil shores of Wailea Beach. This crescent-shaped beach is perfect for swimming, sunbathing, and enjoying the picturesque views. For avid surfers, Ho'okipa Beach Park on the north shore is a must-visit, renowned for its powerful waves and the opportunity to watch talented windsurfers in action.

To further explore the underwater world, indulge in snorkeling or scuba diving excursions to Molokini Crater, a partially submerged volcanic crater offering exceptional visibility and vibrant marine life. Don't miss the chance to encounter sea turtles, tropical fish, and, if you're lucky, even dolphins or humpback whales during the winter months.

Cultural and Historical Sites:
Immerse yourself in Maui's rich history and culture by visiting its numerous cultural and historical sites. Lahaina, the former capital of the Kingdom of Hawaii, is a treasure trove of history. Stroll down Front Street, lined with charming shops and restaurants, and explore the

historic landmarks such as the Baldwin Home Museum and the Lahaina Heritage Museum.

To learn more about Maui's indigenous culture, visit the Maui Arts and Cultural Center in Kahului, where you can enjoy traditional music and dance performances. Attend a luau, a Hawaiian feast accompanied by music and hula dancing, to experience the island's vibrant culture firsthand.

Outdoor Adventures:

Maui offers thrilling outdoor adventures for adrenaline junkies. Take a helicopter tour and witness the island's magnificent landscapes from above, including cascading waterfalls, hidden valleys, and rugged coastlines. If you're up for a challenge, embark on a guided hike along the Pipiwai Trail in the southeastern part of the island, leading you through bamboo forests to the awe-inspiring Waimoku Falls.

For an unforgettable experience, try zip-lining through the lush valleys of Upcountry Maui or go horseback riding along the scenic trails of the island. You can also try your hand at stand-up paddleboarding or kayaking in the calm waters of Makena Bay.

The people of Maui

Maui is the second-largest island in the Hawaiian archipelago and is known for its breathtaking natural beauty, vibrant culture, and warm hospitality. The people of Maui, like all Hawaiians, have a unique cultural heritage that is deeply rooted in the land and sea that surround them. Here is a detailed overview of the people of Maui.

Native Hawaiians:

Native Hawaiians are the indigenous people of Hawaii, including Maui. They have a rich and ancient Polynesian heritage that dates back centuries. The traditional Hawaiian way of life, known as "Hawaiian culture," forms the foundation of their identity. Native Hawaiians have a deep spiritual connection to the land, and they believe that all aspects of nature are interconnected. They have a strong sense of aloha (love), ohana (family), and kuleana (responsibility) to their community and the environment.

Local Residents:

Maui is a multicultural society with a diverse population of residents. Many locals have mixed ancestry, combining Native Hawaiian, Asian, European, and other ethnic backgrounds. The local residents have embraced the aloha spirit and are known for their friendliness and welcoming nature. They take pride in their island home and often participate in community events and cultural celebrations.

Immigrant Communities:

Maui, like the rest of Hawaii, has a significant immigrant population that adds to the cultural tapestry of the island. Various ethnic communities have made Maui their home, including Japanese, Chinese, Filipino, Korean, Portuguese, and Puerto Rican, among others.

These immigrant communities have brought their traditions, customs, and cuisine, contributing to the vibrant multiculturalism of Maui.

Artists and Performers:

Maui has a thriving arts and entertainment scene, attracting artists, musicians, and performers from all over the world. The island is known for its traditional and contemporary Hawaiian music, hula dancing, and storytelling. Many local artists create beautiful works inspired by the island's natural beauty, using mediums such as painting, sculpture, photography, and traditional crafts.

Fishermen and Farmers:

The people of Maui have a deep connection to the land and sea. Fishing and farming have long been essential to their way of life. Traditional fishing techniques, such as throw netting, are still practiced, alongside modern methods. Local fishermen provide the island with a fresh supply of seafood. Similarly, farmers cultivate crops such as taro, sweet potatoes, fruits, and vegetables, both for local consumption and export.

Tourism Industry Workers:

Maui's tourism industry plays a significant role in the local economy, employing a large number of residents. Many people work in hotels, resorts, restaurants, and various tourist attractions. They often interact with visitors, sharing their knowledge of the island's culture and history, and ensuring a memorable experience for tourists.

Environmental Stewards:
Given Maui's breathtaking natural landscapes, the people of Maui are passionate about preserving and protecting their environment. There are numerous community organizations, non-profits, and individuals actively involved in conservation efforts, beach cleanups, and promoting sustainable practices. The people of Maui recognize the importance of living in harmony with nature and are dedicated to preserving their island home for future generations.

In conclusion, the people of Maui represent a diverse and culturally rich community. Native Hawaiians, local residents, immigrant communities, artists, fishermen, farmers, tourism industry workers, and environmental stewards all contribute to the vibrant tapestry of Maui's society. Their shared values of aloha, community, and respect for nature create a unique and welcoming atmosphere for residents and visitors alike.

The rules and regulations

Maui, located in the state of Hawaii, is known for its stunning landscapes, beautiful beaches, and vibrant culture. Like any other destination, Maui has its own set of rules and regulations that visitors and residents must adhere to. Here is a detailed overview of some of the important rules and regulations in Maui:

Beach Rules:

Respect designated swimming areas and follow lifeguards' instructions.
Observe all posted signs and warnings.
Do not disturb or harm marine life, including coral reefs and sea turtles.
Avoid littering and dispose of trash properly.
Fires and camping are generally not allowed on beaches, unless in designated areas.

Water Activities:

Follow safety guidelines and regulations for water activities, such as snorkeling, scuba diving, surfing, and paddleboarding.
Use designated areas for watercraft and observe boating regulations.
Stay away from areas with strong currents or dangerous surf conditions.

Environmental Conservation:

Protect the natural environment and do not damage or remove plants, flowers, rocks, or other natural resources.
Avoid littering and dispose of waste properly in designated trash bins.

Respect protected areas, such as wildlife sanctuaries and nature reserves.
Use reef-safe sunscreen to minimize harm to coral reefs.

Driving and Transportation:

Follow all traffic laws and regulations, including speed limits and seatbelt usage.
Do not drink and drive.
Observe parking regulations and avoid parking in restricted or no-parking zones.
If renting a vehicle, ensure you have a valid driver's license and comply with the rental agreement.

Cultural Etiquette:

Respect the local culture and customs of Maui, including the Hawaiian language and traditions.
Seek permission before entering private property, especially if it has cultural or historical significance.
Be mindful of sacred sites and cultural artifacts, and do not touch or disturb them.
Avoid wearing inappropriate clothing in sacred or religious places.

Wildlife and Nature:

Do not feed or approach wild animals, as it can disrupt their natural behavior and cause harm.

Keep a safe distance from marine mammals, such as dolphins and whales, to avoid distressing them.
Do not touch or harass sea turtles, which are protected under federal and state laws.

Smoking and Vaping:

Smoking and vaping are generally prohibited in public areas, including beaches, parks, and restaurants. Some designated smoking areas may exist.

Noise and Disturbance:

Respect the peace and privacy of residents and other visitors by keeping noise levels to a minimum, especially during quiet hours.
Avoid excessive noise, particularly in residential areas and hotel accommodations.
These are some of the general rules and regulations in Maui. It is important to note that specific rules may vary depending on the location and the activities you engage in. It is always recommended to research and familiarize yourself with any additional regulations applicable to your specific situation to ensure a safe and enjoyable experience on the island.

Accomodations

Maui, a popular Hawaiian island, offers a wide range of accommodations to suit different budgets and preferences. Whether you're looking for luxury resorts, beachfront hotels, cozy bed and breakfasts, or vacation rentals, Maui has something for everyone. Here is a detailed overview of the various types of accommodations you can find in Maui:

Resorts: Maui is known for its luxurious resorts that offer top-notch amenities, breathtaking ocean views, and world-class service. These resorts often feature multiple pools, spas, fitness centers, fine dining restaurants, and direct access to the beach. Some of the well-known resort areas in Maui include Wailea, Ka'anapali, and Kapalua.

Hotels: There are numerous hotels scattered throughout Maui, ranging from budget-friendly options to upscale establishments. Many hotels are located near popular attractions and offer amenities such as swimming pools, on-site restaurants, and concierge services. The main hotel areas in Maui are Lahaina, Kahului, and Kihei.

Vacation Rentals: If you prefer a more private and home-like experience, vacation rentals are a popular choice in Maui. You can find a variety of options including beachfront condos, villas, cottages, and houses. Vacation rentals provide amenities like fully equipped kitchens, multiple bedrooms, and often feature stunning ocean or mountain views. Websites and platforms like Airbnb and VRBO offer a wide selection of vacation rentals in Maui.

Bed and Breakfasts: For a cozy and intimate stay, consider booking a bed and breakfast (B&B) in Maui. B&Bs are typically smaller properties run by local hosts, providing a personalized experience. They often include homemade breakfast and may offer additional amenities like communal areas, gardens, or even private lanais (balconies) with beautiful views.

Camping: If you're an outdoor enthusiast, Maui offers camping opportunities in designated areas. The most popular camping site is the Hosmer Grove Campground in Haleakala National Park, which provides basic facilities and stunning views of the volcanic landscape. Permits are required for camping, and it's essential to be well-prepared with camping gear and supplies.

When choosing accommodations in Maui, it's important to consider factors such as location, proximity to attractions, budget, and desired amenities. It's advisable to book in advance, especially during peak travel seasons, to secure your preferred choice and get the best rates. Additionally, researching customer reviews and comparing options can help you make an informed decision that aligns with your needs and preferences.

Lastly, keep in mind that Maui is a highly popular tourist destination, and accommodations may vary in availability and pricing depending on the time of year.

Affordable accomodations in Maui and where to get them.

Maui, one of the beautiful islands of Hawaii, offers a range of accommodation options to suit different budgets. If you're looking for the cheapest accommodations in Maui, you have several choices, including budget hotels, hostels, vacation rentals, and camping sites. Here is a detailed overview of these options and where you can find them:

Budget Hotels: Maui has a few budget-friendly hotels that offer affordable rates. These hotels typically provide basic amenities such as comfortable rooms, Wi-Fi access, and sometimes a continental breakfast. Some of the affordable hotels in Maui include Maui Beach Hotel, Maui Seaside Hotel, and Lahaina Inn.

Hostels: Hostels are a popular choice for budget travelers, and Maui has a few excellent options. Hostels provide dormitory-style accommodations where you share a room with other travelers. They usually have communal areas where you can socialize and meet fellow travelers. The Maui Hostel in Wailuku and Banana Bungalow Maui Hostel in Lahaina are two well-known hostels on the island.

Vacation Rentals: Renting a vacation home or condo can be a cost-effective option, especially for families or groups traveling together. Websites like Airbnb, VRBO, and HomeAway offer a wide range of affordable vacation rentals in different parts of Maui. You can find options ranging from shared rooms to entire apartments or houses, giving you more space and flexibility during your stay.

Camping: If you enjoy outdoor adventures, camping in Maui can be a great way to save money on accommodation. There are several campgrounds on the island that offer affordable rates and beautiful surroundings. Some popular camping spots include Hosmer Grove Campground in Haleakala National Park, Wai'anapanapa State Park, and Camp Olowalu. Keep in mind that you'll need to bring your own camping gear.

To find the cheapest accommodations in Maui, you can use various resources:

Online Travel Agencies (OTAs): Websites like Expedia, Booking.com, and Hotels.com allow you to search for accommodations based on your budget and preferences. These platforms often provide user reviews, photos, and detailed information about each property.

Local Tourism Websites: Visit the official tourism website for Maui or the Maui Visitors Bureau's website. They often provide a list of accommodations, including budget options, along with contact information and links to their websites.

Vacation Rental Websites: As mentioned earlier, websites like Airbnb, VRBO, and HomeAway offer a wide selection of vacation rentals in Maui. You can filter the results based on price range, location, and other preferences.

Travel Forums and Blogs: Join travel forums or browse through travel blogs where people share their experiences and recommendations for budget-friendly accommodations in Maui. You can find valuable insights and personal recommendations from fellow travelers.

Remember to book in advance, especially during peak travel seasons, as the cheapest accommodations tend to fill up quickly. Be flexible with your travel dates if possible, as rates can vary depending on the time of year.

Chapter 4

Maui culture and custom.

Maui, known as the "Valley Isle," is the second-largest island in the Hawaiian archipelago and is home to a rich and vibrant culture. The cultural heritage of Maui is deeply rooted in the traditions and customs of the native Hawaiian people. Here is a detailed overview of Maui's culture and customs.

Native Hawaiian Roots:
The cultural foundation of Maui stems from the ancient Polynesians who first settled in the Hawaiian Islands. These early settlers brought with them a deep connection to the land and a reverence for nature. The native Hawaiians developed a complex social structure, which included a system of chiefs, priests, warriors, and commoners.

Language:
The Hawaiian language, known as ʻŌlelo Hawaiʻi, plays a significant role in the preservation of Maui's culture. Although English is widely spoken on the island, there has been a concerted effort to revitalize and promote the Hawaiian language. You may encounter Hawaiian words and phrases throughout Maui, and many signs and public announcements include both English and Hawaiian translations.

Hula and Music:

Hula, the traditional Hawaiian dance, is a celebrated art form in Maui. It combines precise movements of the hands, feet, and hips with chanting or singing. Hula is often accompanied by traditional instruments such as the ukulele, guitar, and various percussion instruments. Maui is also renowned for its music scene, with many talented musicians and bands performing a wide range of genres, including traditional Hawaiian music, slack-key guitar, and contemporary island-inspired music.

Cultural Events and Festivals:

Maui hosts numerous cultural events and festivals throughout the year, providing opportunities for both locals and visitors to immerse themselves in the island's culture. One of the most significant events is the annual Maui County Fair, featuring exhibits, rides, entertainment, and a showcase of local crafts and cuisine. Other notable festivals include the Makawao Rodeo, Lahaina's Banyan Tree Ho'olaule'a, and the Aloha Festivals, which are celebrated across the Hawaiian Islands.

Connection to Nature:

The people of Maui have a deep respect and connection to the natural world. The land, ocean, and all living beings are considered sacred. The concept of "āina," which means land, encompasses a holistic understanding of the environment and the interdependence between humans and nature. Practices such as conservation, sustainability, and responsible tourism are embraced to preserve the island's natural beauty.

Ohana and Hospitality:
The concept of "ohana," meaning family, is highly valued in Maui's culture. Family ties extend beyond immediate relatives to include close friends and even the community at large. Visitors to Maui often experience the warmth and hospitality of the locals, who are known for their friendliness and welcoming nature.

Traditional Crafts and Art:
Maui's cultural heritage is also preserved through traditional crafts and art forms. Skilled artisans create intricate works, including wood carvings, featherwork, kapa (bark cloth) making, and traditional lei (garland) making. These crafts not only serve as beautiful expressions of Hawaiian culture but also provide a connection to the ancestral knowledge and traditions passed down through generations.

Cultural Centers and Museums:
Maui is home to several cultural centers and museums dedicated to preserving and promoting Hawaiian culture. The Bailey House Museum in Wailuku showcases artifacts and exhibits that provide insights into Maui's history and cultural practices. The Maui Arts and Cultural Center hosts performances, art exhibitions, and

educational programs, offering a platform for local artists and cultural practitioners.

In summary, Maui's culture and customs are deeply rooted in the traditions of the native Hawaiian people. From hula and music to a strong connection to nature, the people of Maui embrace their cultural heritage and strive to preserve it

Some notable days in Maui.

Maui, the second-largest island in the Hawaiian archipelago, has several notable days and events throughout the year that are celebrated by its residents and visitors. These events showcase the island's rich cultural heritage, natural beauty, and vibrant community spirit. Here is a detailed overview of some notable days on Maui:

Makahiki Season (November - February): Makahiki is an ancient Hawaiian festival that celebrates the harvest and the start of a new year. It typically lasts for several months and includes various cultural and sporting events. During this season, traditional games like konane (Hawaiian checkers), ulu maika (bowling), and moa pahe'e (dart sliding) are played. Makahiki also involves ceremonies, feasts, and offerings to the Hawaiian gods.

Chinese New Year Festival (January/February): The Chinese New Year Festival is a significant celebration for Maui's Chinese community and visitors. The festivities include lion and dragon dances, martial arts performances, cultural displays, fireworks, and delicious Chinese cuisine. The festival often takes place in Lahaina and attracts locals and tourists alike.

Maui Whale Festival (February - March): The annual Maui Whale Festival is a month-long celebration of the magnificent humpback whales that visit the island's waters during the winter months. The festival features various educational and recreational activities, such as whale-watching cruises, marine science presentations, art exhibitions, live music, and a grand parade. It highlights the importance of whale conservation and raises awareness about these majestic creatures.

Maui County Agricultural Festival (April): The Maui County Agricultural Festival, also known as "Ag Fest," is a popular event that showcases the island's diverse agricultural industry. Farmers, ranchers, and local food producers come together to promote sustainable farming practices, share their products, and educate the public about agriculture's significance. The festival offers live entertainment, cooking demonstrations, farm tours, and a range of delicious food and beverages.

Maui Onion Festival (May): Held in the town of Kaanapali, the Maui Onion Festival celebrates the island's famous sweet Maui onions. This lively event features cooking competitions, recipe contests, live music, arts and crafts, and of course, a chance to savor delicious onion-inspired dishes. The festival highlights the unique flavors and versatility of Maui's homegrown onions.

Maui Film Festival (June): The Maui Film Festival is an annual event that celebrates cinema and attracts filmmakers, actors, and movie enthusiasts from around the world. Held in the resort areas of Wailea and Lahaina, the festival showcases a diverse selection of independent and international films, along with red carpet premieres, panel discussions, and awards ceremonies. The stunning outdoor venues provide a magical setting for movie screenings under the stars.

Fourth of July Celebrations: Like the rest of the United States, Maui celebrates Independence Day on July 4th. The island hosts various events, including fireworks displays, parades, live music performances, beach parties, and barbecues. Popular locations for celebrations include Lahaina, Kihei, and Maalaea.

Maui County Fair (September): The Maui County Fair is one of the island's largest annual events, drawing people from all over Maui and neighboring islands. This multi-day fair takes place at the War Memorial Complex in Wailuku and offers a wide range of attractions, including carnival rides, agricultural exhibitions, livestock displays, live entertainment, local food vendors, arts and crafts, and a spectacular fireworks finale.

These notable days and events on Maui showcase the island's vibrant culture, natural wonders, and community spirit. They provide visitors and locals alike with unique opportunities to engage with Maui's rich heritage, connect with the local community, and celebrate the island's beauty and diversity.

Maui days of public holiday.

As of my knowledge cutoff in September 2021, the state of Hawaii, which includes the island of Maui, observes a set of public holidays. These holidays are recognized by the government, and many businesses and schools may be closed or have modified schedules on these days. However, please note that there might have been changes or additional holidays introduced since then, so it's always best to consult up-to-date sources for accurate information.

New Year's Day (January 1st): This is a widely celebrated public holiday across the United States and marks the beginning of the new year. It is a day for rest, reflection, and spending time with family and friends.

Martin Luther King Jr. Day (third Monday in January): This day honors the civil rights leader, Martin Luther King Jr. His contributions and achievements in advancing equality and justice are recognized through various events and activities.

Presidents' Day (third Monday in February): Also known as Washington's Birthday, this holiday commemorates the birthdays of George Washington, the first President of the United States, and Abraham Lincoln, the 16th President. It is a day to honor and remember the contributions of past presidents.

Prince Jonah Kuhio Kalanianaole Day (March 26th): This holiday is specific to the state of Hawaii and celebrates the birth of Prince Jonah Kuhio Kalanianaole, a Hawaiian statesman and delegate to the United States Congress. He is known for his efforts in preserving and promoting Native Hawaiian culture and rights.

Memorial Day (last Monday in May): Memorial Day is a federal holiday dedicated to honoring and remembering the men and women who have died while serving in the United States Armed Forces. It is a day of remembrance and often involves ceremonies, parades, and visits to cemeteries to pay respects.

Independence Day (July 4th): Independence Day celebrates the adoption of the Declaration of Independence in 1776, which declared the United States' independence from British rule. It is a day of patriotic celebration, marked by fireworks, parades, barbecues, and various outdoor activities.

Labor Day (first Monday in September): Labor Day recognizes the contributions and achievements of American workers. It is a day dedicated to the social and economic achievements of the labor movement. Many people enjoy a long weekend and engage in recreational activities.

Veterans Day (November 11th): Veterans Day is a day to honor all military veterans who have served in the United States Armed Forces. It is a time to express gratitude and appreciation for their sacrifices. Ceremonies, parades, and events are held across the country to commemorate veterans' service.

Thanksgiving Day (fourth Thursday in November): Thanksgiving Day is a cherished holiday when families and friends gather to express gratitude and share a festive meal. It traces its origins back to the early pilgrims' harvest feast and is a time for reflection, appreciation, and togetherness.

Christmas Day (December 25th): Christmas is a widely celebrated holiday that commemorates the birth of Jesus Christ. It is a time of joy, gift-giving, and spending time with loved ones. Many people decorate their homes, exchange presents, and attend religious services.

These are the general public holidays observed in the state of Hawaii, including Maui. However, it's essential to note that businesses may have different policies regarding closures or modified hours on these holidays. It's always a good idea to check with local authorities, businesses, or official sources to get accurate information on public holidays specific to Maui or any updates that may have occurred since my knowledge cutoff date.

Cities in Maui and their history.

Maui, a beautiful island in Hawaii, is home to several cities and towns that are rich in history and culture. Let's explore some of the major cities in Maui and delve into their unique pasts.

Kahului:
Kahului is the largest town and the economic hub of Maui. Originally a small fishing village, it experienced significant growth during the sugar plantation era in the late 19th and early 20th centuries. The opening of the Kahului Railroad in 1888 further accelerated its development. Today, Kahului is known for its commercial activities, with bustling shopping centers, the Kahului Harbor, and the Kahului Airport, which serves as the main gateway to Maui.

Lahaina:
Lahaina is a historic town located on the western coast of Maui. In ancient times, it served as a significant Hawaiian royal capital and a thriving center for the whaling industry in the 19th century. Lahaina's Front Street is a picturesque stretch lined with preserved historic buildings, art galleries, boutiques, and restaurants. Visitors can explore landmarks like the

Baldwin House Museum, the Lahaina Courthouse, and the famous Banyan Tree, which is one of the largest in the United States.

Wailuku:
Wailuku, the county seat of Maui County, is situated in the Iao Valley and is known for its lush landscapes and natural beauty. The town was originally settled by Polynesians and later became a hub for sugar production during the plantation era. Today, Wailuku preserves its historic charm with buildings dating back to the 19th century. Notable attractions include the Bailey House Museum, the 'Iao Theater, and the iconic 'Iao Valley State Monument, which features the 'Iao Needle, a striking rock pinnacle.

Kihei:
Kihei is a popular resort town located on the southwestern coast of Maui. It started as a small fishing village but experienced significant growth in the 20th century. Kihei is renowned for its stunning beaches, crystal-clear waters, and year-round sunny weather. The town offers an array of water activities such as snorkeling, swimming, and surfing. Additionally, visitors can explore the ancient Hawaiian fishponds of Ko'ie'ie and indulge in the vibrant nightlife and dining scene along South Kihei Road.

Makawao:
Nestled on the slopes of Haleakala Volcano, Makawao is a charming upcountry town with a rich history in

paniolo (Hawaiian cowboy) culture. Originally a ranching community, Makawao still retains its western ambiance with its rustic wooden storefronts and art galleries. The annual Makawao Rodeo is a popular event that showcases traditional Hawaiian horsemanship and roping skills. The town is also known for its Paniolo Parade, held during the Fourth of July celebrations.

These are just a few examples of the cities and towns in Maui, each with its own unique history and character. Whether you're interested in the island's plantation past, ancient Hawaiian heritage, or its stunning natural beauty, Maui offers a diverse range of experiences that capture the essence of this enchanting Hawaiian island.

Chapter 5

General security situation

Maui General Security is a reputable security company that specializes in providing a wide range of security services to businesses, organizations, and individuals on the island of Maui, Hawaii. With a strong commitment to protecting people and property, Maui General Security has established itself as a trusted provider of comprehensive security solutions

overview of Maui General Security:

Services:
Maui General Security offers a comprehensive suite of security services tailored to meet the unique needs of its clients. Some of the key services provided include:

a. **Security Guard Services**: The company provides highly trained and professional security guards who are skilled in various aspects of security, including access control, patrolling, and emergency response. These guards are deployed to safeguard properties, monitor premises, and ensure the safety and well-being of clients.

b. **Event Security**: Maui General Security has expertise in event security management, offering crowd control, access control, perimeter security, and VIP protection services for events of all sizes. Their team of security professionals ensures that events run smoothly and safely.

c. Alarm Systems and Monitoring: The company installs and maintains alarm systems, including intrusion detection systems, video surveillance, and fire alarms. They also provide 24/7 monitoring services to promptly respond to any alarms triggered, ensuring a swift and efficient emergency response.

d. Mobile Patrols: Maui General Security offers mobile patrol services, utilizing marked vehicles and experienced security personnel to conduct regular patrols of properties. This proactive approach helps deter criminal activities and ensures a visible security presence.

e. Executive Protection: For clients requiring personal protection services, Maui General Security provides highly trained and experienced executive protection agents who ensure the safety and security of individuals at all times.

f. Consulting and Risk Assessment: The company offers security consulting services to assess vulnerabilities, identify risks, and develop customized security plans for businesses and organizations. These assessments help clients enhance their security measures and minimize potential threats.

Team and Training:

Maui General Security takes pride in its team of security professionals who undergo rigorous training to meet industry standards. The company recruits individuals with relevant backgrounds, such as law enforcement or military experience, and provides ongoing training to ensure their skills are up-to-date. This training covers areas such as emergency response, conflict resolution, surveillance techniques, and customer service, enabling the team to deliver exceptional security services.

Technology and Partnerships:

Maui General Security leverages advanced security technologies and partnerships with leading industry providers to deliver effective security solutions. They utilize state-of-the-art alarm systems, video surveillance cameras, access control systems, and other cutting-edge tools to enhance the overall security of their clients' properties. Through strategic partnerships, the company can offer comprehensive security solutions that integrate technology, personnel, and expertise.

Customer Focus:

Maui General Security places a strong emphasis on customer satisfaction. They work closely with their clients to understand their unique security needs and tailor solutions accordingly. The company maintains open lines of communication, ensuring clients receive regular updates and prompt responses to their inquiries. By providing personalized and reliable security services,

Maui General Security aims to build long-term relationships with its clients based on trust and exceptional service.

In summary, Maui General Security is a leading security company on the island of Maui, Hawaii, offering a wide range of services including security guards, event security, alarm systems, mobile patrols, executive protection, consulting, and risk assessments. With a focus on professionalism, expertise, and customer satisfaction, Maui General Security is dedicated to ensuring the safety and security of its clients and their properties.

Emergency and important numbers you must know.

In Maui, Hawaii, there are several emergency and important numbers that residents and visitors should be aware of. These numbers are crucial for reporting emergencies, seeking assistance, or obtaining important information. Here is a detailed list of emergency and important numbers in Maui:

Emergency Services:

Police Emergency: 911
Fire Emergency: 911
Medical Emergency: 911
Non-Emergency Services:

Maui Police Department: +1 (808) 244-6400
Maui Fire Department: +1 (808) 270-7566
American Medical Response (Ambulance): +1 (808) 244-2991
Maui Civil Defense Agency:

Maui County Civil Defense Agency: +1 (808) 270-7285
This agency provides information and updates on natural disasters, severe weather conditions, and other emergencies.
Hospitals and Medical Centers:

Maui Memorial Medical Center: +1 (808) 244-9056
Kula Hospital: +1 (808) 878-1221
Maui Health System: +1 (808) 442-5100
These medical facilities provide emergency medical care, trauma services, and general healthcare.
Poison Control:

Hawaii Poison Hotline: +1 (800) 222-1222
In case of accidental poisoning, contact this hotline for immediate assistance and guidance.
Coast Guard:

U.S. Coast Guard - Maui Station: +1 (808) 893-6421
This number can be used for reporting maritime emergencies, boating accidents, or distress situations at sea.
Roadside Assistance:

AAA Hawaii: +1 (800) 222-4357

For vehicle breakdowns or roadside emergencies, contact this number for assistance.
Utilities:

Maui Electric Company: +1 (808) 871-9777
Hawaiian Telcom (Phone, Internet, Cable): +1 (808) 643-3456
These numbers are useful for reporting power outages, utility issues, or seeking support related to phone and internet services.
Visitor Information:

Maui Visitors Bureau: +1 (808) 244-3530
This number provides information about tourist attractions, accommodations, and general inquiries for visitors to Maui.
It is important to note that emergency numbers should be used solely for genuine emergencies requiring immediate assistance. Misusing emergency services can result in delays for individuals in genuine need. Non-emergency numbers should be utilized for general inquiries or situations that do not require immediate attention.

Beaches in Maui

Maui, one of the islands in Hawaii, is known for its stunning beaches that attract visitors from all over the world. With its pristine white sands, crystal-clear waters, and breathtaking scenery, Maui offers a wide range of beach experiences for every type of traveler. Here is a detailed overview of some of the best beaches in Maui:

Ka'anapali Beach: Located on the western shore of Maui, Ka'anapali Beach is one of the most popular and iconic beaches on the island. With three miles of golden sand, this beach offers excellent swimming and snorkeling opportunities. The beach is lined with luxury resorts, restaurants, and shops, making it a vibrant and lively destination. Black Rock, a prominent lava formation at the northern end of the beach, is a popular spot for cliff jumping and snorkeling.

Wailea Beach: Situated on the southwestern coast of Maui, Wailea Beach is known for its luxurious resorts and calm, clear waters. The beach boasts soft golden sand and provides a peaceful and relaxing atmosphere. Snorkeling and swimming are popular activities here, and visitors can often spot sea turtles swimming near the shore. The beach is also home to a paved oceanfront path known as the Wailea Beach Path, offering scenic views and access to other beautiful beaches in the area.

Kapalua Bay Beach: Considered one of the best beaches in the United States, Kapalua Bay Beach is located on Maui's northwestern coast. The beach is tucked between two rocky points, creating a sheltered and calm bay perfect for swimming, snorkeling, and paddleboarding. The waters here are teeming with vibrant marine life, including tropical fish and coral reefs. The beach offers ample shade from palm trees and is surrounded by lush greenery, adding to its natural beauty.

Napili Bay: Just north of Kapalua Bay, Napili Bay is a picturesque crescent-shaped beach with golden sand and turquoise waters. The bay is sheltered by two rocky points, creating calm and gentle waves. Snorkeling is excellent here, as the bay is home to a vibrant coral reef and a variety of marine life. The beach has a laid-back atmosphere, with a few resorts and condominiums nearby. It is a great spot for sunbathing, swimming, and enjoying stunning sunsets.

Hookipa Beach Park: Located on Maui's north shore, Hookipa Beach Park is renowned for its powerful waves and is a favorite destination for experienced surfers and windsurfers. The beach is also known for its strong winds, making it a popular spot for kiteboarding. Even if you're not into water sports, Hookipa offers spectacular views of the ocean and is an ideal place to observe sea turtles and catch a glimpse of humpback whales during the winter months.

Makena Beach State Park: Often referred to as "Big Beach," Makena Beach State Park is a vast stretch of golden sand situated on Maui's southern shore. The beach is known for its stunning beauty and spaciousness, offering plenty of room for sunbathing, beach games, and long walks along the shoreline. The waters can be rough at times, so caution is advised for swimming. Adjacent to Big Beach is "Little Beach," a clothing-optional beach popular among the alternative community.

Hamoa Beach: Located in the small town of Hana on Maui's eastern coast, Hamoa Beach is a hidden gem known for its natural beauty and seclusion. The beach is surrounded by lush green cliffs and boasts soft, golden sand and clear turquoise waters. The waves here can be a bit stronger, making it a great spot for bodyboarding and bodysurfing. Hamoa Beach offers a tranquil escape and is often less crowded compared to the

Entertainments in Maui.

Maui, often referred to as the "Valley Isle," is a beautiful and vibrant island in Hawaii known for its stunning beaches, lush landscapes, and rich cultural heritage. When it comes to entertainment, Maui offers a diverse range of options to cater to every taste and interest. Whether you're looking for live performances, outdoor adventures, or cultural experiences, Maui has something for everyone. Here is a detailed overview of entertainment options in Maui:

Hula Shows: One of the most iconic forms of entertainment in Hawaii is the traditional hula dance. Maui showcases this ancient Polynesian art form through various hula shows held throughout the island. The shows often include skilled dancers, live music, and vibrant costumes, providing an immersive cultural experience.

Luaus: Attending a traditional Hawaiian luau is a must-do activity in Maui. These festive celebrations combine Hawaiian cuisine, music, dance, and storytelling. Luaus typically feature a buffet-style feast with traditional dishes like kalua pork, poi, and haupia (coconut pudding). Guests can enjoy live music, fire knife performances, hula dances, and even participate in arts and crafts activities.

Maui Arts and Cultural Center: Located in Kahului, the Maui Arts and Cultural Center is the premier venue for performing arts on the island. It hosts a wide range of events, including concerts, theatrical performances, dance shows, and art exhibitions. The center features multiple performance spaces, including an outdoor amphitheater, and attracts both local and international artists.

Water Activities: Maui's stunning beaches and crystal-clear waters offer numerous entertainment opportunities. Snorkeling and scuba diving allow you to explore vibrant coral reefs teeming with marine life. You can also try paddleboarding, kayaking, or take sailing tours to discover the island's breathtaking coastline. Whale watching is another popular activity during the winter months when humpback whales migrate to the warm Hawaiian waters.

Road to Hana: The Road to Hana is a scenic highway that winds through Maui's lush rainforests, waterfalls, and dramatic coastal cliffs. This 64-mile road trip is an adventure in itself, with plenty of stops along the way to explore waterfalls, botanical gardens, and black sand beaches. It's a great way to immerse yourself in Maui's natural beauty and enjoy outdoor entertainment.

Maui Ocean Center: Located in Maalaea, the Maui Ocean Center is a fantastic destination for families and ocean enthusiasts. It is home to a vast collection of marine life, including sharks, turtles, tropical fish, and coral reefs. The center offers interactive exhibits, educational presentations, and even opportunities to dive with sharks or participate in behind-the-scenes tours.

Maui Film Festival: If you're a movie lover, the annual Maui Film Festival is an event not to be missed. Held in Wailea, the festival showcases a selection of films from around the world, including premieres and award-winning movies. Attendees can enjoy outdoor screenings under the stars, participate in filmmaker panels, and celebrate cinema in a beautiful tropical setting.

Live Music: Throughout Maui, you'll find numerous venues, bars, and restaurants that offer live music performances. From local Hawaiian bands playing traditional music to contemporary artists performing a variety of genres, you can immerse yourself in the island's vibrant music scene. Some popular spots for live music include Lahaina, Kihei, and Paia.

Festivals and Events: Maui hosts a variety of festivals and events throughout the year, celebrating everything from music and art to food and culture. The Maui Onion Festival, Maui Jazz & Blues Festival, and the Maui County Fair are just a few examples of the exciting events that take place annually. These festivals provide a chance to enjoy live performances, sample local cuisine,

Roles of the Maui government towards the immigrant.

The government of Maui, like other local governments in the United States, plays a crucial role in addressing the needs and concerns of immigrants within its jurisdiction. Maui is part of the state of Hawaii and operates under the legal framework and policies established at the federal, state, and local levels. Here are some of the key roles and responsibilities of the Maui government towards immigrants:

Legal Framework: The Maui government ensures that its policies and practices align with federal and state laws concerning immigration. It operates within the parameters set by immigration laws, including those related to visas, residency, and naturalization.

Services and Support: The government of Maui provides various services and support systems to assist immigrants in integrating into the community. This includes access to education, healthcare, social services, and other essential programs.

Language Assistance: Recognizing the linguistic diversity among immigrants, the Maui government may offer language assistance programs to help individuals with limited English proficiency access government services and participate in civic life. This can involve translation services, bilingual staff, and multilingual resources.

Community Outreach: Maui's government plays an important role in fostering inclusivity and engaging with immigrant communities. They may organize community outreach programs, cultural events, and workshops to promote understanding, bridge cultural gaps, and build relationships between immigrants and other residents.

Advocacy and Representation: The government of Maui may advocate for the rights and well-being of immigrants at the local, state, and federal levels. This can include lobbying for comprehensive immigration reform, supporting policies that protect immigrant rights, and representing the interests of immigrants in various forums.

Collaboration with Community Organizations: Maui's government often collaborates with community-based organizations, non-profits, and advocacy groups that specialize in immigrant services. This collaboration can help leverage resources, provide additional support, and ensure a coordinated approach to addressing the needs of immigrants.

Immigration Enforcement: While immigration enforcement is primarily the responsibility of federal agencies such as Immigration and Customs Enforcement (ICE), local law enforcement agencies on Maui may collaborate with federal authorities to enforce immigration laws. However, the extent of involvement in immigration enforcement can vary depending on local policies and priorities.

Access to Legal Resources: The Maui government may facilitate access to legal resources and information for immigrants. This can involve partnerships with legal aid organizations or pro bono services to provide assistance with immigration applications, documentation, and other legal matters.

Employment and Economic Opportunities: The Maui government can contribute to the economic integration of immigrants by fostering an environment that promotes employment opportunities, job training programs, and entrepreneurship. This can involve supporting workforce development initiatives and encouraging inclusive economic policies.

Educational Initiatives: The government of Maui recognizes the importance of education in the integration process. They may implement programs that address the unique needs of immigrant students, such as English as a Second Language (ESL) instruction, cultural competency training for teachers, and inclusive curriculum development.

It is important to note that the specific roles and approaches of the Maui government towards immigrants can evolve over time, influenced by changing policies, community needs, and political climate.

<u>What to do before leaving Maui.</u>

Before leaving Maui, there are several important tasks and considerations to ensure a smooth departure and wrap up your stay on the island. Here is a detailed list of things to do before leaving Maui:

Check your travel documents: Verify that you have your passport, identification, airline tickets, and any other necessary travel documents. Ensure they are valid and readily accessible.

Confirm your travel arrangements: Double-check your flight details, including departure time, terminal, and any potential changes. If you have transportation booked to the airport, reconfirm the pick-up time and location.

Pack and organize your belongings: Begin packing your luggage and organize your belongings. Make a checklist to ensure you haven't forgotten anything important. Consider leaving extra space in your luggage for any souvenirs or purchases you might make before departure.

Settle outstanding bills: Before leaving your accommodations, settle any outstanding bills, such as hotel charges, rental car fees, or vacation rental payments. Ensure you have accounted for any additional charges or fees that may have accrued during your stay.

Return rented equipment: If you have rented any equipment, such as snorkeling gear, surfboards, or bicycles, return them to the rental company and settle any remaining payments or deposits.

Empty the refrigerator and pantry: If you have been staying in a vacation rental or self-catering accommodation, clear out any perishable items from the refrigerator and pantry. Dispose of any leftovers and properly clean the kitchen.

Return keys and access cards: If you have been provided with keys or access cards for your accommodation, return them to the front desk or rental agency as instructed. Ensure you haven't forgotten any keys for vehicles or lockboxes.

Check out of your accommodation: Coordinate with the front desk or rental agency to officially check out of your accommodation. Follow any specific procedures they may have, such as settling final payments, returning key cards, or conducting a room inspection.

Cancel or redirect services: If you have subscribed to any local services, such as newspaper delivery, mail forwarding, or temporary gym memberships, make arrangements to cancel or redirect them. Notify any relevant providers of your departure date.

Clear out personal items: Ensure you haven't left any personal belongings behind in your accommodation. Double-check closets, drawers, and bathroom cabinets. Don't forget to retrieve any chargers, adapters, or electronics you may have used during your stay.

Return rental vehicles: If you have rented a car, motorcycle, or any other type of vehicle, return it to the rental agency in the agreed-upon condition and time. Fill up the gas tank if required, remove any personal belongings, and settle any remaining payments or fees.

Withdraw cash and settle accounts: Visit a local bank or ATM to withdraw sufficient cash for your immediate needs, such as airport expenses or transportation upon arrival at your next destination. Settle any outstanding bills or debts you may have incurred during your stay.

Check the weather and prepare for the journey: Check the weather forecast for both Maui and your destination. Pack appropriate clothing and accessories, taking into account any climate or seasonal differences.

Say goodbye and express gratitude: If you have made connections or friendships during your time in Maui, take the time to say goodbye and express your gratitude to the people who have made your stay enjoyable. Consider leaving a positive review or recommendation for any establishments or services you particularly enjoyed.

Enjoy your final moments: Before leaving the island, take some time to savor the natural beauty and unique experiences that Maui offers. Visit a favorite beach, take a final hike, or enjoy a memorable meal. Create lasting memories to cherish from your time in Maui.

By following these steps and taking care of necessary tasks, you can ensure a hassle-free departure from Maui.

Conclusions.

In conclusion, the "Travel Guide to Maui" offers a comprehensive and informative resource for anyone planning a trip to this beautiful Hawaiian island. The book provides a wealth of detailed information, practical tips, and insider recommendations to ensure a memorable and enriching experience on Maui. Throughout its pages, the guide showcases the island's diverse attractions, stunning landscapes, vibrant culture, and enticing activities.

One of the standout features of the guide is its meticulous attention to detail. The book covers every aspect of planning a trip, from pre-travel preparations and booking accommodations to exploring Maui's must-see sights and hidden gems. Whether it's deciding when to visit, understanding the local customs and etiquette, or navigating transportation options, the guide offers invaluable advice to help readers make the most of their time on the island.

The book's organization is logical and user-friendly, allowing readers to easily navigate between different sections and find the information they need. The guide divides Maui into distinct regions, such as Lahaina, Hana, and Upcountry, providing comprehensive insights into each area's unique attractions, landmarks, and activities. By structuring the content in this manner, the guide allows travelers to plan their itinerary based on their interests and preferences.

Moreover, the "Travel Guide to Maui" stands out for its in-depth exploration of Maui's natural wonders. The book devotes considerable attention to the island's breathtaking beaches, lush rainforests, cascading waterfalls, and volcanic landscapes. It provides detailed descriptions of popular beach spots, along with lesser-known alternatives that offer solitude and tranquility. The guide also includes tips on snorkeling, scuba diving, hiking trails, and other outdoor adventures, catering to both adventure seekers and nature enthusiasts.

Another notable aspect of the guide is its emphasis on cultural immersion. It sheds light on Maui's rich heritage, traditions, and local customs, encouraging readers to engage with the island's cultural offerings. From attending traditional Hawaiian luaus to visiting historic sites and exploring art galleries, the guide offers suggestions to deepen one's understanding and appreciation of Maui's vibrant culture.

The inclusion of practical information and helpful resources is also commendable. The guide provides essential details on transportation options, dining recommendations, shopping opportunities, and safety tips, ensuring that readers are well-equipped to navigate Maui with ease and convenience. Additionally, the book incorporates maps, suggested itineraries, and contact information for various services, further enhancing its usefulness as a practical travel companion.

Overall, the "Travel Guide to Maui" is a highly valuable resource for travelers planning a trip to this tropical paradise. With its comprehensive coverage, attention to detail, and practical advice, the guide empowers readers to create their own unique and unforgettable experiences on the island. Whether one seeks adventure, relaxation, cultural exploration, or a combination of these, this travel guide serves as an excellent companion, offering insights and recommendations that will enhance any Maui vacation.

Made in the USA
Las Vegas, NV
09 December 2023

82457627R00046